Henry
the Rain

Written by Jill Eggleton
Illustrated by Rob Kiely

Henry looked
out the window.
It was raining.

"**Go away, Rain!**"
he shouted.
"I like the sun."

3

The rain came in the windows.

It came under the door.

It came down the chimney.
Drip, drip, drip!

7

Henry went to get the mop.

But he went into a puddle.

"**Look at me, Rain!**"
he shouted.
"I'm wet!"

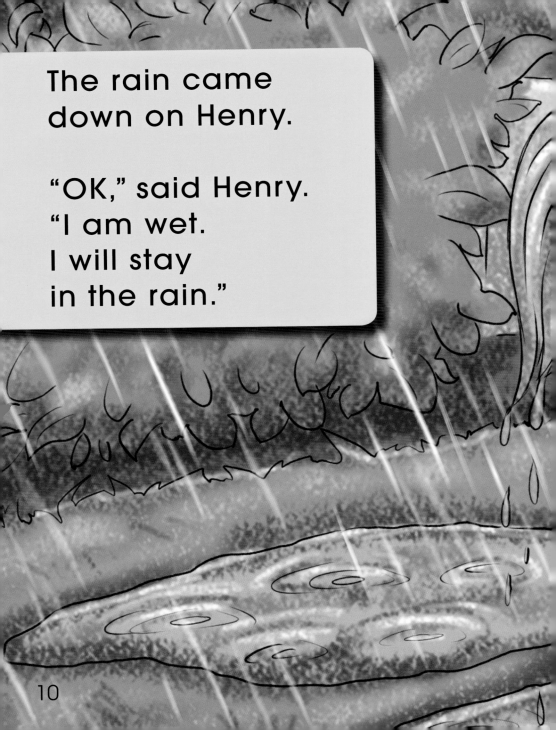

The rain came
down on Henry.

"OK," said Henry.
"I am wet.
I will stay
in the rain."

10

Henry went in
the puddles – *splosh!*

He went in
the mud – *splosh!*

"This is fun!" said Henry.
And he danced with the mop!

13

A Flow Diagram

Guide Notes

Title: Henry and the Rain
Stage: Early (2) – Yellow

Genre: Fiction
Approach: Guided Reading
Processes: Thinking Critically, Exploring Language, Processing Information
Written and Visual Focus: Flow Diagram
Word Count: 127

THINKING CRITICALLY
(sample questions)
- What do you think this story could be about?
- Focus on the title and discuss.
- How do you know the rain is a nuisance for Henry?
- Why do you think Henry changed his mind about the rain?
- What do you think people might have said if they had seen Henry out in the rain?
- What do you think Henry might do now that the sun is out?

EXPLORING LANGUAGE

Terminology
Title, cover, illustrations, author, illustrator

Vocabulary
Interest words: rain, drip, mop, splosh, danced
High-frequency words: stay, with, all
Positional words: under, into, down, out, in, up

Print Conventions
Capital letter for sentence beginnings and names (**H**enry), full stops, commas, quotation marks, exclamation marks